J

D0773765

21st Century
Basic Skills
Library

KIDS CAN
KEEP WATER CLEAN

by Cecilia Minden, PhD

Cherry Lake Publishing • Ann Arbor, Michigan

3

Published in the United States of America
by Cherry Lake Publishing
Ann Arbor, Michigan
www.cherrylakepublishing.com

Photo Credits: Cover and page 1, ©Jeff Greenberg/Alamy; page 4, ©hkannn/Shutterstock, Inc.; page 6, ©Vibrant Image Studio/Shutterstock, Inc.; page 8, ©Jaimie Duplass/Shutterstock, Inc.; page 10, ©Tonis Valing/Shutterstock, Inc.; page 12, ©riekephotos/Shutterstock, Inc.; page 14, ©teekaygee/Shutterstock, Inc.; page 16, ©Robert Rozbora/Shutterstock, Inc.; page 18, ©Lifestyle/Alamy; page 20, ©OJO Images Ltd/Alamy

Library of Congress Cataloging-in-Publication Data
Minden, Cecilia.
  Kids can keep water clean/by Cecilia Minden.
    p. cm.—(Kids can go green!)
  Includes index.
  ISBN-13: 978-1-60279-872-4 (lib. bdg.)
  ISBN-10: 1-60279-872-9 (lib. bdg.)
  1. Water—Pollution—Juvenile literature. 2. Water quality—Juvenile literature. 3. Water quality management—Juvenile literature. I. Title.
  TD370.M556 2011
  363.739'4—dc22   2009049743

Cherry Lake Publishing would like to acknowledge the work of The Partnership for 21st Century Skills.
Please visit *www.21stcenturyskills.org* for more information.

Printed in the United States of America
Corporate Graphics Inc.
July 2010
CLFA07

TABLE OF CONTENTS

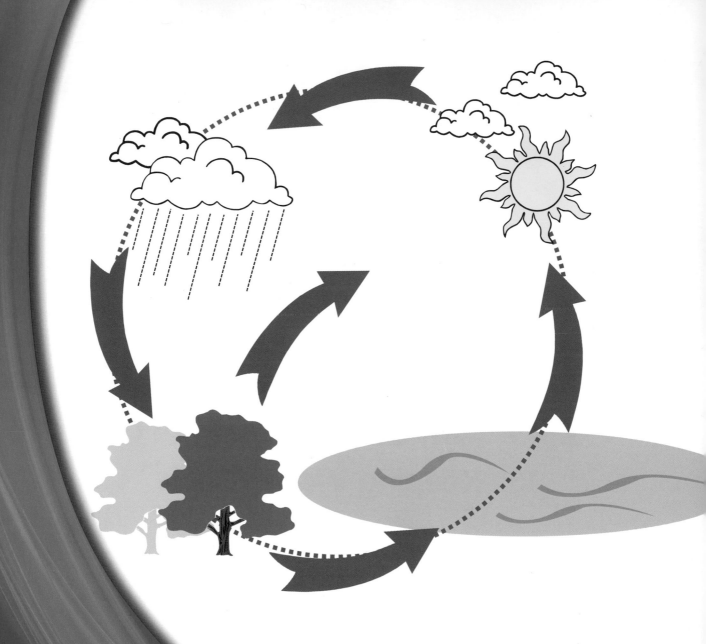

Where Does Water Come From?

Earth's water goes around and around in a **water cycle**.

The hot sun heats water on Earth. Water becomes **steam**. The steam rises into the air.

Air high above Earth is cold. The cold air turns steam into clouds.

Rain falls when clouds cannot hold any more water. The rain fills up lakes and rivers.

Why Should Water Be Clean?

More than half of our bodies are made of water.

We need clean water to stay alive.

Dirty water also hurts plants and animals.

Animals and plants become sick. Some will die.

Keeping Water Clean

Stop! Think before putting something in a **drain**.

Drains carry things to our **water supply**. Only safe things should go in drains.

Always read labels. Choose **products** that are safe for our water.

Learn the best ways to **dispose** of things that can hurt our water.

Don't flush trash down a **toilet**. The trash goes into our water.

Use safe products on plants. Some **plant sprays** can hurt the water.

Do you like to play outside?

Clean up your trash!

Wind and rain can blow trash into the water.

Share with others what you've learned about clean water. Work together to think of other ways you can help.

What will you do today to keep water clean?

Find Out More

BOOK

Knight, M.J. *Why Should I Turn Off the Tap?* Mankato, MN: Smart Apple Press, 2009.

WEB SITE

US EPA—Drinking Water & Ground Water Kids' Stuff
www.epa.gov/OGWDW/kids/kids_k-3.html
Play games and do activities to help you learn about water.

Glossary

drain (DRAYN) an opening to pipes that take away water

dispose (diss-POZE) to throw away something you are done using

plant sprays (PLANT SPRAYZ) chemicals put on plants to help them grow

products (PROD-uhkts) things made to be used by people

steam (STEEM) vapor formed when water is heated

toilet (TOI-lit) a large bowl that can be flushed with water to dispose of wastes from the human body

water cycle (WAW-tur SYE-kuhl) the constant movement of Earth's water

water supply (WAW-tur suh-PLYE) a source of water

Home and School Connection

Use this list of words from the book to help your child become a better reader. Word games and writing activities can help beginning readers reinforce literacy skills.

a	carry	for	like	share	turns
about	choose	from	made	should	up
above	clean	go	more	sick	use
air	clouds	goes	need	some	water
alive	cold	half	of	something	ways
also	come	heats	on	sprays	we
always	cycle	help	only	stay	what
and	die	high	other	steam	when
animals	dirty	hold	others	stop	where
any	dispose	hot	our	sun	why
are	do	hurt	outside	supply	will
around	does	hurts	plant	than	wind
be	don't	in	plants	that	with
become	down	into	play	the	work
becomes	drain	is	products	things	you
before	drains	keep	putting	think	your
best	Earth	keeping	rain	to	you've
blow	Earth's	labels	read	today	
bodies	falls	lakes	rises	together	
can	fills	learn	rivers	toilet	
cannot	flush	learned	safe	trash	

23

Index

About the Author

Cecilia Minden is the former Director of the Language and Literacy Program at the Harvard Graduate School of Education. She currently works as a literacy consultant for school and library publishers and is the author of more than 100 books for children.

24